# LION AND THE LAMB

90-day Blessings
Daily Devotional and Journal

Vol. 1

INGRID D STUBBS

Copyright © 2015 Ingrid D. Stubbs

All rights reserved. No part of this book may be used or reproduced by any means, graphic, electronic, or mechanical, including photocopying, recording, taping or by any information storage retrieval system without the written permission of the author except in the case of brief quotations embodied in critical articles and reviews.

Scripture taken from the New King James Version. Copyright © 1982 by Thomas Nelson, Inc. Used by permission. All rights reserved.

Scripture taken from the Holy Bible, American Standard Version, copyright © 1901. Public domain.

Scripture taken from The Holy Bible, NEW INTERNATIONAL VERSION® NIV®. Copyright © 1973, 1978, 1984 by International Bible Society®. Used by permission. All rights reserved worldwide.

Scripture quotations taken from the Holy Bible, New Living Translation, copyright ©1996, 2004, 2007, 2013 by Tyndale House Foundation. Used by permission of Tyndale House Publishers, Inc., Carol Stream, Illinois 60188. All rights reserved.

Scripture quotations taken from the Amplified® Bible, Copyright © 1954, 1958, 1962, 1964, 1965, 1987 by The Lockman Foundation. Used by permission. (www.Lockman.org)

Year of the Book
135 Glen Avenue
Glen Rock, PA 17327

Cover Design by Pixelstudio

ISBN 13: 978-1-942430-46-9

ISBN 10: 1-942430-46-9

Library of Congress Control Number: 2015957023

# ACKNOWLEDGEMENTS:

This book is dedicated to my late Pastor, Dr. Ronald L. Leonard. He has inspired me throughout my entire Christian walk. He and his wife Gloria adopted me as their spiritual daughter. He taught me to love the Lord with all my heart and soul no matter what was going on in my life. He taught me the most important things in my life should always be the Word of God, and my personal relationship with Jesus Christ. He taught and walked the Word of God every moment of his life.

He always believed in me, and for this I am forever grateful. He encouraged me to teach my children about the Lord as early as possible. Today my children are 12 and 15, they are on fire for Jesus and have learned to put their faith in God. My husband George continues to encourage me in all my endeavors. I also would like to thank my Pastors, Tony & Liz Townsend, my daddy James C. Phillip, my mother Agnes Hutchinson who is my best friend and encourager and my father Wingrove Hutchinson, who is always there for me.

And also to: Constantia Pemberton, Millicent Liburd, Albertine Burrell, Myrna Hooker, James Morton, Livingston Herbert, Ermaine Morris, Sylvester Herbert, Lauren Rivers, Ken Pemberton, Walford Pemberton, Mervin Pemberton, Jennifer Haliger, Anthony Chapman, Vera Hanley, Sylvia Cornelius, David Clarke, Vernon Phillip, Shelly Ann Phillip, Andrea Phillip-Capleton, Steven Phillips, Winston K. Phillips, Gweneth Henry, Jacinth Caines, Erney Clarke, Shermaine Clarke, Katrina Clark, Angela Phillip-Francis, Julia Rowe, Eleanor Leak, and my entire family.

# INTRODUCTION

I was inspired to write this book by a New Year's sermon from my pastor, Tony Townsend, who encouraged us to focus on the many blessings in our lives rather than the negatives.

For more than a year, I put this into practice in my own life. At the end of each day, I sat down and wrote about all the amazing things that had happened. There were far more blessings to be thankful for than circumstances that discouraged me. The practice of noticing good things in my life gave me joy that came from positive thinking—and even more reasons to be grateful.

As we focus on the smallest blessings throughout the day, we will begin to see life in a new light and it's not all bad.

A small blessing could be finding a parking space close to the store, especially if your feet are hurting from working overtime. Overtime is also a blessing because it creates extra money you would not have originally had. A big blessing could be an unexpected check in the mail to pay your taxes, or a good report from the doctors.

In each day of this journal, read the scripture passage. As you think about its meaning for your life, you can create a prayer for yourself. Then read the "Gratitude." Take time to reflect on your day and—rather than dwelling on the negatives—make a list of all the blessings.

# TODAY IS A GIFT FROM GOD!

## (A PRESENT)

## TOMORROW MAY NEVER COME!

## Our Greatest Need is Salvation

For with the heart man believeth unto righteousness; and with the mouth confession is made unto salvation.

For whosoever shall call upon the name of the Lord shall be saved.

—Romans 10:10,13 (KJV)

## Prayer for Salvation:

Dear Lord Jesus,

Come into my heart. I repent for my sins and all I've done wrong. I believe you died on the cross for my sins and God raised Jesus from the dead on the third day. Cleanse me and change me; live your life in me. I turn my back on the world, I turn my back on sin. Fill me with your Holy Spirit and set me free. Thank you for forgiving me; I am saved and I have eternal life with you. Give me a passion for the lost and for the things of you, God. Help me to fulfill all you have ordained me to do. In Jesus mighty name, Amen!

## LIVE EACH DAY WITH AN ATTITUDE OF GRATITUDE

Be thankful for the small things!

Begin each day with a prayer and end each day thanking God for his blessings.

# Day 1

## God Knows You

---

Before I formed you in the womb I knew you; before you were born I sanctified you; and I ordained you a prophet to the nations.

—Jeremiah 1: 5 (NKJV)

Prayer:

_____

_____

_____

_____

_____

_____

_____

_____

Gratitude: Lord, I thank you that you knew me before I was born; I am not an accident.

# Today's Blessings

# Day 2

## God Has a Plan For You

---

For I know the thoughts that I think towards you, says the Lord, thoughts of peace, and not of evil, to give you a future and a hope.

—Jeremiah 29: 11 (NKJV)

Prayer:

_____
_____
_____
_____
_____
_____
_____
_____

Gratitude: Thank you, Lord, that you have good plans for my life.

# Today's Blessings

# Day 3

## God Has Put Us In Charge of the Earth

---

Then God said, "Let Us make man in Our image, according to Our likeness; let them have dominion over the fish of the sea, over the birds of the air, over the cattle, over all the earth and over every creeping thing that creeps on the earth."

—Genesis 1:26 (NKJV)

Prayer:

_____
_____
_____
_____
_____
_____

Gratitude: Thank you, Lord, that I am made in your image, therefore I have authority over everything.

# Today's Blessings

# Day 4

## Everything God Made is Good

---

Then God saw everything that He had made, and indeed it was very good. So the evening and morning were the sixth day.

—Genesis 1:31 (NKJV)

Prayer:

_____

_____

_____

_____

_____

_____

_____

_____

Gratitude: Lord, you made me, so therefore I am good in your sight.

# Today's Blessings

# Day 5

## Your Family is Blessed

---

Blessing I will bless you, and multiplying I will multiply your descendants as the stars of heaven and as the sand which is on the seashore; and your descendants shall possess the gate of their enemies.

—Genesis 22:17 (NKJV)

Prayer:

_____

_____

_____

_____

_____

_____

_____

_____

Gratitude: Lord, thank you for the blessings on my family from generation to generation.

# Today's Blessings

# Day 6

## You Are Blessed

---

You are sons of the prophets, and of the covenant which God made with our fathers, saying to Abraham, and in your seed all the families of the earth shall be blessed.

—Acts 3:25 (NKJV)

Prayer:

_____

_____

_____

_____

_____

_____

_____

_____

Gratitude: Thank you, Lord, that I have been blessed from the seeds of my ancestors.

# Today's Blessings

# Day 7

## Take Time to Rest

Then God blessed the seventh day and made it holy, because on it he rested from all the work of creating that he had done.

—Genesis 2:3 (NIV)

Prayer:

_____

_____

_____

_____

_____

_____

_____

_____

Gratitude: Lord, help me to take time to rest from all my work and not to be a workaholic.

# Today's Blessings

# Day 8

## Obey God's Voice

---

In your seed all the nations of the earth shall be blessed, because you have obeyed My voice.

—Genesis 22:18 (NKJV)

Prayer:

_____

_____

_____

_____

_____

_____

_____

_____

Gratitude: Lord, thank you that I will obey your voice and see your blessings.

# Today's Blessings

# Day 9

## Have a Willing Heart

---✦◉ ⁂ ◉✦---

If you are willing and obedient, you shall eat the good of the land: But if you refuse and rebel, you shall be devoured by the sword; for the mouth of the Lord has spoken.

—Isaiah 1:19-20 (NKJV)

Prayer:

_____
_____
_____
_____
_____
_____
_____
_____

Gratitude: Thank you, Lord, I choose to be willing and obedient and will not rebel against you.

# Today's Blessings

# Day 10

## Help Each Other

---

Two are better than one; because they have a good reward for their labor. For if they fall, one will lift up his companion. But woe to him who is alone when he falls, for he has no one to help him up.

—Ecclesiastes 4:9-10 (NKJV)

Prayer:

_____
_____
_____
_____
_____
_____
_____

Gratitude: Thank you, Lord, that I can help others up when they are down, therefore, I will be helped in my time of need.

# Today's Blessings

# Day 11

## Don't Be Prideful

A man's pride will bring him low, but the humble in spirit will retain honor.

—Proverbs 29:23 (NKJV)

Prayer:

_____
_____
_____
_____
_____
_____
_____
_____

Gratitude: Lord, I will be humble for you and not prideful.

# Today's Blessings

# Day 12

## Don't Let Sin Rule

---•◦ ⚬◦⚬ ◦•---

He who covers his sin will not prosper, but whosoever confesses and forsakes them will have mercy.

—Proverbs 28:13 (NKJV)

Prayer:

_____
_____
_____
_____
_____
_____
_____
_____

Gratitude: Thank you, Lord, that I will confess all my sins before you.

# Today's Blessings

# Day 13

## Don't Envy Others

---

Do not be envious of evil men, nor desire to be with them.

—Proverbs 24:1 (NKJV)

Prayer:

_____
_____
_____
_____
_____
_____
_____
_____

Gratitude: Thank you that the spirit of envy does not have place in my life.

# Today's Blessings

# Day 14

## God Knows Our Motives

The Lord's light penetrates the human spirit, exposing every hidden motive.

—Proverbs 20:27 (NLT)

Prayer:

_____
_____
_____
_____
_____
_____
_____
_____
_____

Gratitude: Lord, search every hidden motive in me.

# Today's Blessings

# Day 15

## God Will Make You Prosperous

Then Isaac sowed in that land and reaped in the same year a hundredfold; and the Lord blessed him. The man began to prosper, and continued prospering until he became very prosperous.

—Genesis 26:12-13 (NKJV)

Prayer:

_____
_____
_____
_____
_____
_____
_____
_____

Gratitude: Thank you, Lord, that I am reaping and prospering because I have sown.

# Today's Blessings

# Day 16

## May the Lord Be With You

---

The Lord was with Joseph, and he was a successful man; and he was in the house of his master the Egyptian. And his master saw the Lord was with him and that the Lord made all he did to prosper in his hand.

—Genesis 39:2-3 (NKJV)

Prayer:

_____
_____
_____
_____
_____
_____
_____
_____

Gratitude: Thank you, Lord, that you are with me.

# Today's Blessings

# Day 17

## The Lord Will Fight For You

---

"The Lord will fight for you, and you shall hold your peace."

—Exodus 14:14 (NKJV)

Prayer:

_____

_____

_____

_____

_____

_____

_____

_____

Gratitude: Thank you, Lord, that you fight all my battles; I don't have to do it myself.

# Today's Blessings

# Day 18

## The Lord Heals

---

He said, "If you will listen carefully to the voice of the Lord your God and do what is right in his sight, obeying his commands and keeping all his decrees, then I will not make you suffer any of the diseases I sent on the Egyptians, for I am the Lord who heals you."

—Exodus 15:26 (NLT)

Prayer:

_____

_____

_____

_____

_____

_____

_____

Gratitude: I am healed from all diseases because I keep your commands.

# Today's Blessings

# Day 19

## God is With You Wherever You Go

---

"Behold, I am with you and will keep you wherever you go, and will bring you back to this land; for I will not leave you until I have done what I have spoken to you."

—Genesis 28:15 (NKJV)

Prayer:

_____

_____

_____

_____

_____

_____

_____

_____

Gratitude: Lord, you will never leave me.

# Today's Blessings

# Day 20

## God Will Preserve You

The Lord shall preserve your going out and your coming in from this time forth, and even forevermore.

—Psalm 121:8 (NKJV)

Prayer:

_____
_____
_____
_____
_____
_____
_____
_____
_____

Gratitude: I thank you, Lord, for preserving me forever.

# Today's Blessings

# DAY 21

## FAITH COMES BY HEARING AGAIN AND AGAIN

---

So then faith comes by hearing and hearing by the Word of God.

—Romans 10:17 (NKJV)

Prayer:

_____

_____

_____

_____

_____

_____

_____

Gratitude: Thank you, Lord, that my faith is growing because I'm hearing your Word.

# Today's Blessings

# Day 22

## We Have God's Promise

Therefore it is of faith that it might be according to grace, so that the promise might be sure to all the seed, not only to those who are of the law, but also to those who are of the faith of Abraham, who is the father of us all.

—Romans 4:16 (NKJV)

Prayer:

_____

_____

_____

_____

_____

_____

_____

Gratitude: Thank you, Lord. Because of your promise to Abraham, I too have your promise.

# Today's Blessings

# Day 23

## We Inherit Eternal Life

Because of his grace he declared us righteous and gave us confidence that we will inherit eternal life.

—Titus 3:7 (NLT)

Prayer:

_____

_____

_____

_____

_____

_____

_____

_____

Gratitude: Lord, I thank you for your grace so I have inherited eternal life.

# Today's Blessings

# Day 24

## Live in Freedom

---

For you have been called to live in freedom, my brothers and sisters. But don't use your freedom to satisfy your sinful nature. Instead, use your freedom to serve one another in love.

—Galatians 5:13 (NLT)

Prayer:

_____

_____

_____

_____

_____

_____

_____

Gratitude: Thank you, Lord, that I gain freedom by serving others in love.

# Today's Blessings

# Day 25

## Give Glory to His Name

---

Give to the Lord the glory due His name; bring an offering, and come before Him. Oh, worship the Lord in the beauty of holiness!

—1 Chronicles 16:29 (NKJV)

Prayer:

_____

_____

_____

_____

_____

_____

_____

Gratitude: Lord, I will worship you and glorify your holy name.

# Today's Blessings

# Day 26

## Spirit and Truth

---

God is a Spirit: and they that worship him must worship him in spirit and in the truth.

—John 4:24 (KJV)

Prayer:

_____
_____
_____
_____
_____
_____
_____
_____
_____
_____

Gratitude: Father, I worship you with my whole heart.

# Today's Blessings

# Day 27

## Stay Connected

---

If you abide in Me, and My words abide in you, you will ask what you desire, and it shall be done for you.

—John 15:6 (NKJV)

Prayer:

_____
_____
_____
_____
_____
_____
_____
_____
_____

Gratitude: Thank you, Lord, because I am abiding in your word and I am receiving what I desire.

# Today's Blessings

# Day 28

## Help Those in Need

Give to the one who asks you, and do not turn away from the one who wants to borrow from you.

—Matthew 5:42 (NIV)

Prayer:

_____

_____

_____

_____

_____

_____

_____

_____

Gratitude: Lord, give me compassion to always help those in need.

# Today's Blessings

# Day 29

## Rejoice and Reverence the Lord

---

Praise the Lord! Blessed is the man who fears the Lord, who delights greatly in His commandments.

—Psalm 112:1 (NKJV)

Prayer:

_____

_____

_____

_____

_____

_____

_____

Gratitude: Lord, I delight in your word and I am rejoicing in you.

# Today's Blessings

# Day 30

## We Can't Give Up

---

Therefore, since God in his mercy has given us this new way, we never give up.

—2 Corinthians 4:1 (NLT)

Prayer:

_____
_____
_____
_____
_____
_____
_____
_____
_____

Gratitude: Help me, Lord, to never give up on you and your promises.

# Today's Blessings

# Day 31

## Look Beyond Our Troubles

So we don't look at the troubles we can see now; rather, we fix our gaze on things that cannot be seen. For the things we see now will soon be gone, but the things we cannot see will last forever.

—2 Corinthians 4:18 (NLT)

Prayer:

_____
_____
_____
_____
_____
_____
_____
_____

Gratitude: Thank you, Lord, that my troubles will not last forever.

# Today's Blessings

# Day 32

## The Blood of Jesus

---

And from Jesus Christ, who is the faithful witness, and the first begotten of the dead, and the prince of the kings of the earth. Unto him that loved us, and washed us from our sins in his own blood, and hath made us kings and priests unto God and his Father; to him be glory and dominion forever and ever. Amen.

—Revelation 1:5-6 (KJV)

Prayer:

_____

_____

_____

_____

_____

_____

Gratitude: Thank you, Lord, that we are made to be kings and priests unto God, my sins are forgiven, and you love me, shown by the shedding of your blood.

# Today's Blessings

# Day 33

## The Love and Mercy of God

Guard and keep yourselves in the love of God; expect and patiently wait for the mercy of our Lord Jesus Christ the Messiah, which will bring you unto eternal life.

—Jude 21 (AMP)

Prayer:

_____

_____

_____

_____

_____

_____

_____

Gratitude: Lord, I keep myself in your love, expecting your mercies to keep me safe which gives me eternal life.

# Today's Blessings

# Day 34

## Faithfully

---

Faithful is he that called you, who also will do it.

—1 Thessalonians 5:24 (KJV)

Prayer:

_____
_____
_____
_____
_____
_____
_____
_____
_____
_____

Gratitude: Father, you are faithful in all your ways.

# Today's Blessings

# Day 35

## Be Holy

Because it is written, "Be holy, for I am holy."

—1 Peter 1:16 (NKJV)

Prayer:

_____
_____
_____
_____
_____
_____
_____
_____
_____

Gratitude: Lord, I declare I will walk in a spirit of holiness.

# Today's Blessings

# Day 36

## Jesus Died For Us

For God so loved the world that He gave His only begotten Son, that whoever believes in Him should not perish but have eternal life. For God did not send His Son into the world to condemn the world, but that the world through Him might be saved.

—John 3:16-17 (NKJV)

Prayer:

_____

_____

_____

_____

_____

_____

_____

Gratitude: Thank you, Lord. You love me so much you sent your only son to die for me so I can be saved.

# Today's Blessings

# Day 37

## Vengeance is the Lord's

---

You shall not take vengeance, nor bear any grudge against the children of your people, but you shall love your neighbor as yourself: I am the Lord.

—Leviticus 19:18 (NKJV)

Prayer:

_____

_____

_____

_____

_____

_____

_____

_____

Gratitude: I will not take vengeance, it belongs to you, Lord; but I will love others like I love myself.

# Today's Blessings

# Day 38

## Love is Action

My little children, let us not love in word neither in tongue, but in deed and in truth.

—1 John 3:18 (NKJV)

Prayer:

_____

_____

_____

_____

_____

_____

_____

_____

Gratitude: I will show love by my actions, not just by my words.

# Today's Blessings

# Day 39

## Love God with All of You

---

You shall love the Lord your God with all your heart, with all your soul, and with all your strength.

—Deuteronomy 6:5 (NKJV)

Prayer:

_____

_____

_____

_____

_____

_____

_____

_____

_____

Gratitude: I will love you, Lord, with all of my being.

# Today's Blessings

# Day 40

## Always Be Loyal

A friend is always loyal, and a brother is born to help in time of need.

—Proverbs 17:17 (NLT)

Prayer:

_____
_____
_____
_____
_____
_____
_____
_____
_____

Gratitude: I thank you, Lord, that I am a true friend.

# Today's Blessings

# Day 41

## God is Love

---

Dear friends, let us continue to love one another, for love comes from God. Anyone who loves is a child of God. But anyone who does not love does not know God, for God is love.

—1 John 4:7 (NKJV)

Prayer:

_____
_____
_____
_____
_____
_____
_____
_____

Gratitude: I can love others because I know God.

# Today's Blessings

# Day 42

## Everything Has Its Time

---

A time to love, and a time to hate.

—Ecclesiastes 3:8 (NLT)

Prayer:

_____
_____
_____
_____
_____
_____
_____
_____
_____
_____

Gratitude: Lord, help me to know your seasons, because there is a time for everything.

# Today's Blessings

# Day 43

## Love Your Enemies

---

But I say to you, love your enemies, bless those who curse you, do good to those who hate you, and pray for those who spitefully use you and persecute you.

—Matthew 5:44 (NKJV)

Prayer:

_____

_____

_____

_____

_____

_____

_____

Gratitude: I choose to love my enemies and pray for those who hate me.

# Today's Blessings

# Day 44

## No Fear In Love

There is no fear in love. But perfect love drives out fear, because fear has to do with punishment. The one who fears is not made perfect in love.

—1 John 4:18 (NIV)

Prayer:

Gratitude: I will love and not fear.

# Today's Blessings

# Day 45

## Waiting on Jesus Gives Us Strength

---

Wait on the Lord; be of good courage, and He shall strengthen your heart; wait, I say, on the Lord!

—Psalm 27:14 (NKJV)

Prayer:

_____
_____
_____
_____
_____
_____
_____
_____

Gratitude: Lord, I thank you that I have the courage to wait on you and you strengthen me daily.

# Today's Blessings

# Day 46

## God Delights in Blessing Us

But give great joy to those who came to my defense. Let them continually say, "Great is the Lord, who delights in blessing his servant with peace!"

—Psalm 35:27 (NLT)

Prayer:

_____

_____

_____

_____

_____

_____

_____

Gratitude: Lord, you delight in blessing me with your peace and I am grateful.

# Today's Blessings

# Day 47

## Obedience Leads to Righteousness

---

Because one person disobeyed God, many became sinners. But because one other person obeyed God, many will be made righteous.

—Romans 5:19 (NLT)

Prayer:

_____

_____

_____

_____

_____

_____

_____

Gratitude: Thank you, Lord. Because of my obedience to God, I am made righteous.

# Today's Blessings

# Day 48

## Honesty is the Best Policy

An honest answer is like a kiss of friendship.

—Proverbs 24:26 (NLT)

Prayer:

_____

_____

_____

_____

_____

_____

_____

_____

_____

Gratitude: Lord, I choose to be honest with all my answers even if it hurts. Dishonesty ruins relationships.

# Today's Blessings

# Day 49

## Godly Mindset

Set your mind on the things above, not on earthly things.

—Colossians 3:2 (NIV)

Prayer:

___

___

___

___

___

___

___

___

Gratitude: Thank you that I have the mind of Christ and my mind is fixed on the godly things, not what I see with my natural eyes.

# Today's Blessings

# Day 50

## All Things Are Possible With God

---

Jesus looked at them and said, "With man this is impossible, but not with God; all things are possible with God."

—Mark 10:27 (NIV)

Prayer:

_____

_____

_____

_____

_____

_____

_____

Gratitude: Thank you, Lord, that I believe with you *all* things are possible!

# Today's Blessings

# Day 51

## We Live By Your Word

---

And Jesus had fasted forty days and forty nights, afterward He was hungry. Now when the tempter came to Him, he said, "If You are the Son of God, command that these stones become bread." But Jesus answered and said, "It is written, 'Man shall not live by bread alone, but by every word that proceeds from the mouth of God.'"

—Matthew 4:2-4 (NKJV)

Prayer:

_____

_____

_____

_____

_____

_____

Gratitude: Lord, I will feed my spirit with your word and not just my flesh with natural food.

# Today's Blessings

# Day 52

## Faith Produces Patience

---

My brethren, count it all joy when you fall into various trials; knowing that the testing of your faith produces patience. But let patience have its perfect work, that you may be perfect and complete, lacking nothing.

—James 1:2-3 (NKJV)

Prayer:

_____

_____

_____

_____

_____

_____

_____

_____

Gratitude: Thank you, Lord, that patience is being produced in me by activating my faith.

# Today's Blessings

# Day 53

## Love Covers All

Hatred stirs up quarrels, but love makes up for all offenses.

—Proverbs 10:12 (NLT)

Prayer:

_____

_____

_____

_____

_____

_____

_____

_____

_____

Gratitude: I choose to love and not hate.

# Today's Blessings

# Day 54

## Show We Belong to God

"By this all will know that you are My disciples, if you have love for one another."

—John 13:35 (NKJV)

Prayer:

_____

_____

_____

_____

_____

_____

_____

_____

Gratitude: I will show love to everyone because I am your disciple.

# Today's Blessings

# Day 55

## Continue in Love

---

Let brotherly love continue.

—Hebrews 13:1 (KJV)

Prayer:

_____
_____
_____
_____
_____
_____
_____
_____
_____
_____

Gratitude: I will always love my brothers and sisters in Christ.

# Today's Blessings

# Day 56

## Examine Your Heart

---

Keep your heart with all diligence, for out of it springs the issues of life.

—Proverbs 4:23 (NKJV)

Prayer:

_____

_____

_____

_____

_____

_____

_____

_____

Gratitude: I will guard my heart and mind, being watchful of what goes in because it will determine what comes out.

# Today's Blessings

# Day 57

## Shine Bright

But the path of the just is like the shining sun, that shines ever brighter unto the perfect day.

—Proverbs 4:18 (NKJV)

Prayer:

_____
_____
_____
_____
_____
_____
_____
_____
_____

Gratitude: Because I am righteous, Lord, let my light shine brighter each day.

# Today's Blessings

# Day 58

## Knowledge is Power

---

But also for this very reason, giving all diligence, add to your faith virtue, to virtue knowledge, to knowledge self-control, to self-control perseverance, to perseverance godliness, to godliness brotherly kindness, and to brotherly kindness love. For if these things are yours and abound, you will be neither barren nor unfruitful in the knowledge of our Lord Jesus Christ.

—2 Peter 1:5-8 (NKJV)

Prayer:

_____

_____

_____

_____

_____

_____

_____

Gratitude: Thank you, Lord, that because of my knowledge of you, I am growing in all areas of my life.

# Today's Blessings

# Day 59

## Everlasting Love

---

The Lord appeared to us in the past, saying: "I have loved you with an everlasting love; I have drawn you with unfailing kindness."

—Jeremiah 31:3 (NIV)

Prayer:

_____
_____
_____
_____
_____
_____
_____
_____

Gratitude: Thank you, Lord, that your love is everlasting, your kindness is unfailing and you continually draw me to you.

# Today's Blessings

# DAY 60

## FIRST LOVE

We love him, because he first loved us.

—1 John 4:19 (KJV)

Prayer:

_____
_____
_____
_____
_____
_____
_____
_____
_____
_____

Gratitude: You loved me first, therefore, I will love you in return.

# Today's Blessings

# Day 61

## God Still Loves the Backslider

I will heal their backsliding, I will love them freely, for My anger has turned away from him.

—Hosea 14:4 (NKJV)

Prayer:

_____

_____

_____

_____

_____

_____

_____

_____

Gratitude: Lord, thank you for loving me when I have backslidden. You are not angry with me, and you continue to love me freely.

# Today's Blessings

# Day 62

## Restoration

In his kindness God called you to share in his eternal glory by means of Christ Jesus. So after you have suffered a little, he will restore, support, and strengthen you, and he will place you on a firm foundation.

—1 Peter 5:10 (NLT)

Prayer:

_____
_____
_____
_____
_____
_____
_____

Gratitude: Thank you, Lord, that you will restore me, strengthen me and support me because of your kindness.

# Today's Blessings

# Day 63

## God is Merciful

Therefore, be merciful, just as your Father is also merciful.

—Luke 6:36 (NKJV)

Prayer:

_____
_____
_____
_____
_____
_____
_____
_____

Gratitude: Lord, you are compassionate, sympathetic and have tender mercies towards me, and so I desire to be like you.

# Today's Blessings

# Day 64

## Compassion for Us

When the Lord saw her, his heart went out to her and he said, "Don't cry."

—Luke 7:13 (NIV)

Prayer:

_____
_____
_____
_____
_____
_____
_____
_____
_____

Gratitude: Thank you, Lord, for the compassion that you have towards me. When I hurt, you hurt also.

# Today's Blessings

# Day 65

## Confess Jesus to Others

Every one therefore who shall confess me before men, him will I also confess before my Father who is in heaven.

—Matthew 10:32 (ASV)

Prayer:

___

___

___

___

___

___

___

___

Gratitude: I shall confess you daily so others will know I belong to you.

# Today's Blessings

# Day 66

## Please God, Not Man

---

Take heed that you do not do your charitable deeds before men, to be seen by them. Otherwise you have no reward from your Father in heaven.

—Matthew 6:1 (NKJV)

Prayer:

_____
_____
_____
_____
_____
_____
_____
_____

Gratitude: I desire to please you alone, Lord.

# Today's Blessings

# Day 67

## Joy Gives Us Strength

---

Then he said to them, "Go your way, eat the fat, drink the sweet and send portions to those for whom nothing is prepared; for this is holy to our Lord. Do not sorrow, for the joy of the Lord is your strength."

—Nehemiah 8:10 (NKJV)

Prayer:

_____
_____
_____
_____
_____
_____
_____
_____

Gratitude: Thank you, Lord, for when I'm joyful and have renewed strength.

# Today's Blessings

# Day 68

## God is Rejoicing Over Me

---

The Lord your God in your midst, the Mighty One, will save; He will rejoice over you with gladness, He will quiet you with His love, He will rejoice over you with singing."

—Zephaniah 3:17 (NKJV)

Prayer:

_____
_____
_____
_____
_____
_____
_____
_____

Gratitude: Lord, you are Almighty, your love is peaceful. You rejoice over me, therefore, I am grateful.

# Today's Blessings

# Day 69

## Praises to Your Name

---

It is good to give thanks to the Lord, and to sing praises to Your name, O Most High; to declare Your lovingkindness in the morning, and Your faithfulness every night.

—Psalm 92:1-2 (NKJV)

Prayer:

_____

_____

_____

_____

_____

_____

_____

Gratitude: I will praise you in the morning when I get up and I will praise you at night when I lay down.

# Today's Blessings

# DAY 70

## THE HOLY SPIRIT LEADS US

"But the Helper, the Holy Spirit, whom the Father will send in My name, He will teach you all things, and bring to your remembrance all things that I said to you."

—John 14:26 (NKJV)

Prayer:

_____

_____

_____

_____

_____

_____

_____

Gratitude: Thank you, Lord, for the leading and prompting of the Holy Spirit.

# Today's Blessings

# Day 71

## Peace of God

---

Peace I leave with you; my peace I give you. I do not give to you as the world gives. Do not let your hearts be troubled and do not be afraid.

—John 14:27 (NIV)

Prayer:

_____

_____

_____

_____

_____

_____

_____

_____

Gratitude: Lord, I thank you for your peace, I don't have to be afraid, and I am trusting in you.

# Today's Blessings

# Day 72

## Lord, I Need You

---

As the deer longs for streams of water, so I long for you, O God.

—Psalm 42:1 (NLT)

Prayer:

_____
_____
_____
_____
_____
_____
_____
_____
_____

Gratitude: Lord, my heart longs for you. I need you daily to survive.

# Today's Blessings

# Day 73

## Lord, You Are My Helper

---

God is our refuge and strength, a very present help in trouble.

—Psalm 46:1 (NKJV)

Prayer:

_____
_____
_____
_____
_____
_____
_____
_____
_____

Gratitude: Thank you, Lord, that you always help me in times of trouble and uncertainty.

# Today's Blessings

# Day 74

## Lord, You Are Great

---

GREAT is the Lord, and greatly to be praised in the city of our God, in His holy mountain.

—Psalm 48:1 (NKJV)

Prayer:

_____

_____

_____

_____

_____

_____

_____

_____

_____

Gratitude: I praise you, Lord. I love you, Lord. You are great and greatly to be praised!

# Today's Blessings

# DAY 75

## LORD, YOU ARE MY PROTECTOR

He who dwells in the secret place of the Most High shall abide under the shadow of the Almighty. I will say of the Lord, "He is my refuge and my fortress, My God, in Him I will trust."

—Psalm 91:1-2 (NKJV)

Prayer:

_____
_____
_____
_____
_____
_____
_____
_____

Gratitude: Thank you, Lord, for your protection; there is safety in your presence.

# Today's Blessings

# Day 76

## My Confidence Is In God

---

Be still, and know that I am God; I will be exalted among the nations, I will be exalted in the earth.

—Psalm 46:10 (NKJV)

Prayer:

_____
_____
_____
_____
_____
_____
_____
_____

Gratitude: Lord, I honor you. I exalt you, I reverence you. I wait patiently on you.

# Today's Blessings

# DAY 77

## GENERATIONS HAVE TRUSTED YOU

---

Lord, you have been our dwelling place in all generations.

—Psalm 90:1 (NKJV)

Prayer:

_____
_____
_____
_____
_____
_____
_____
_____

Gratitude: Lord, for generations our confidence has been in you and we will continue to trust you for generations to come.

# Today's Blessings

# DAY 78

## HEAR MY PRAYER

---

O Lord, God of my salvation, I have cried out day and night before You. Let my prayer come before You; incline Your ear to my cry.

—Psalm 88:1-2 (NKJV)

Prayer:

_____
_____
_____
_____
_____
_____
_____
_____

Gratitude: Lord, thank you for hearing my prayer. You've seen my tears and you know my fears.

# Today's Blessings

# Day 79

## Never Give Up

---

That is why we never give up. Though our bodies are dying, our spirits are being renewed every day. For our present troubles are small and won't last very long. Yet they produce for us a glory that vastly outweighs them and will last forever!

—2 Corinthians 4:16-17 (NLT)

Prayer:

_____

_____

_____

_____

_____

_____

Gratitude: Lord, troubles may come, but they won't last. I will draw strength from the Holy Spirit, and I won't give up or give in.

# Today's Blessings

# DAY 80

## GOD'S WORD IS FOREVER

---

The grass withers, the flowers fades, but the word of our God stands forever.

—Isaiah 40:8 (NKJV)

Prayer:

_____
_____
_____
_____
_____
_____
_____
_____

Gratitude: Lord, your word will never fade away, so I will believe in your Word that is lasting and nothing else.

# Today's Blessings

# Day 81

## God's Strength and Power

---

He gives strength to the weary and increases the power of the weak.

—Isaiah 40:29 (NIV)

Prayer:

_____

_____

_____

_____

_____

_____

_____

_____

Gratitude: Lord, when I am weak and weary, you give me strength and power to endure and I say "Thank you."

# Today's Blessings

# Day 82

## Comfort and Hope

---

May our Lord Jesus Christ our Father, who loves us and in his special favor gave us everlasting comfort and good hope, comfort your hearts and give you strength in every good thing you do and say.

—2 Thessalonians 2:16-17 (NLT)

Prayer:

_____
_____
_____
_____
_____
_____
_____

Gratitude: Lord, you are comforting me. Thank you for your love and favor—you are watching over the things I do and say.

# Today's Blessings

# Day 83

## Hidden in God

---

Seek the Lord, all you meek of the earth, who have upheld His justice. Seek righteousness, seek humility. It may be that you will be hidden in the day of the Lord's anger.

—Zephaniah 2:3 (NKJV)

Prayer:

_____
_____
_____
_____
_____
_____
_____

Gratitude: Lord, hide me from your anger. Let me continue to seek you and walk in righteousness and humility.

# Today's Blessings

# Day 84

## Unfailing Love

---

Praise God, who did not ignore my prayer and did not withdraw his unfailing love from me.

—Psalm 66:20 (NLT)

Prayer:

_____
_____
_____
_____
_____
_____
_____
_____
_____

Gratitude: Thank you, Lord, for your unfailing love towards me, even if I strayed from you.

# Today's Blessings

# Day 85

## Today I Rejoice

---

This is the day the Lord has made; we will rejoice and be glad in it.

—Psalm 118:24 (NKJV)

Prayer:

_____
_____
_____
_____
_____
_____
_____
_____

Gratitude: Lord, because you have given me today, it is another day I can rejoice and be thankful.

# Today's Blessings

# Day 86

## Humble and Pray

If my people who are called by My name will humble themselves, and pray and seek My face, and turn from their wicked ways, then I will hear from heaven, and will forgive their sin and heal their land.

—2 Chronicles 7:14 (NKJV)

Prayer:

_____
_____
_____
_____
_____
_____
_____
_____

Gratitude: Lord, I humble myself, I ask for forgiveness, I repent and I seek you continually.

# Today's Blessings

# Day 87

## See that God is Good

---

Oh, taste and see that the Lord is good; blessed is the man who trusts in Him!

—Psalm 34:8 (NKJV)

Prayer:

_____

_____

_____

_____

_____

_____

_____

_____

_____

Gratitude: Lord, you are good!

# Today's Blessings

# Day 88

## God's Love Lasts Forever

---

Three things will last forever—faith, hope, and love—and the greatest of these is love.

—1 Corinthians 13:13 (NLT)

Prayer:

_____
_____
_____
_____
_____
_____
_____
_____
_____

Gratitude: Thank you, Lord, your love is the greatest thing in my life and it will last forever!

# Today's Blessings

# DAY 89

## SEASONS ARE INEVITABLE

To everything there is a season, a time for every purpose under heaven.

—Ecclesiastes 3:1 (NKJV)

Prayer:

_____

_____

_____

_____

_____

_____

_____

_____

Gratitude: Lord, I know every season in my life is necessary and essential to fulfil my purpose.

# Today's Blessings

# Day 90

## Renewed Strength

---

But those who trust in the Lord will find new strength; they soar on wings like eagles. They will run and not grow weary, they will walk and not faint.

—Isaiah 40:31 (NLT)

Prayer:

_____

_____

_____

_____

_____

_____

_____

Gratitude: Lord, thank you that I am finding renewed strength in you. I will not grow weary or faint, because I'm trusting in you.

# Today's Blessings

FOCUS ON THE MANY

BLESSINGS

IN YOUR LIFE

# ALSO BY THIS AUTHOR:

Available in print and eBook

www.ingramcontent.com/pod-product-compliance
Lightning Source LLC
LaVergne TN
LVHW051831080426
835512LV00018B/2819